WHAT ARE FOSSIL FUELS?

Coal, oil, and gas are called fossil fuels because they're made from the buried remains of prehistoric plants and animals. These fuels are rich in carbon. When we burn fossil fuels, the stores of carbon that they hold are released into the air as carbon dioxide.

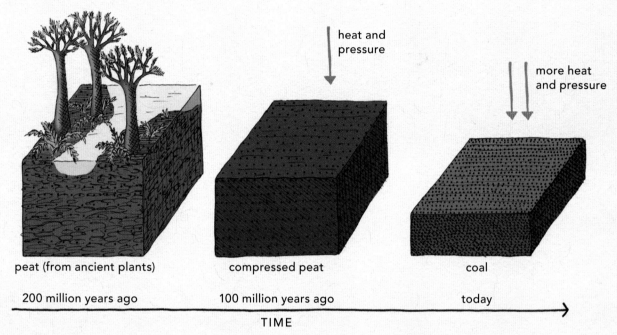

heat and pressure

more heat and pressure

peat (from ancient plants)	compressed peat	coal
200 million years ago	100 million years ago	today

TIME

THE GREENHOUSE EFFECT

The Earth's atmosphere absorbs warmth from the sun; it's called the "greenhouse effect." Carbon dioxide and other gases in the atmosphere that trap heat are called "greenhouse gases." Without the greenhouse effect, the Earth would be much too cold for human life. But when these gases reach excessive levels, the atmosphere traps too much heat. The result is climate change, which is harmful to human and other life.

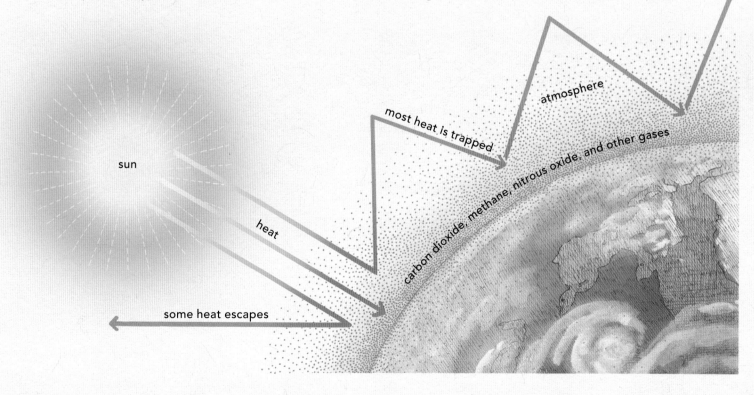

atmosphere

most heat is trapped

sun

carbon dioxide, methane, nitrous oxide, and other gases

heat

some heat escapes

To the change makers, protectors, and innovators —D.L.

For the scientists and activists of the future —A.B.

I am so grateful to Dr. Asmeret Asefaw Berhe, Dr. Samantha Chapman, and Bailey Moritz for their thoughtful reviews of the manuscript that became this book. Any errors remain my own.
—D.L.

BLOOMSBURY CHILDREN'S BOOKS
Bloomsbury Publishing Inc., part of Bloomsbury Publishing Plc
1385 Broadway, New York, NY 10018

BLOOMSBURY, BLOOMSBURY CHILDREN'S BOOKS, and the Diana logo
are trademarks of Bloomsbury Publishing Plc

First published in the United States of America in March 2024
by Bloomsbury Children's Books

Bloomsbury Publishing Plc does not have any control over, or responsibility for, any third-party websites
referred to or in this book. All internet addresses given in this book were correct at the time of going to press.
The author and publisher regret any inconvenience caused if addresses have changed or sites have ceased
to exist, but can accept no responsibility for any such changes.

Bloomsbury books may be purchased for business or promotional use.
For information on bulk purchases please contact
Macmillan Corporate and Premium Sales Department at specialmarkets@macmillan.com

Library of Congress Cataloging-in-Publication Data
available upon request
ISBN 978-1-5476-1206-2 (hardcover) • ISBN 978-1-5476-1207-9 (e-book) • ISBN 978-1-5476-1208-6 (e-PDF)

Art created with pen on paper and digital color
Typeset in Avenir LT Std
Book design by Jeanette Levy
Printed in China by Leo Paper Products, Heshan, Guangdong
2 4 6 8 10 9 7 5 3 1

To find out more about our authors and books visit
www.bloomsbury.com and sign up for our newsletters.

CHANGE
IS IN THE
AIR

Carbon, Climate, Earth, and Us

Debbie Levy • illustrated by Alex Boersma

BLOOMSBURY
CHILDREN'S BOOKS
NEW YORK LONDON OXFORD NEW DELHI SYDNEY

Carbon.

It's in you.
It's in the Earth, it's in the air.
Carbon is in every living thing!

It's also in coal and oil and gas—

fuels formed long ago, underground,
from plants and animals that once were living things.

When we burn those fossil fuels
for heat, electricity, cars, trucks, and planes,
the carbon in them

gushes into the air.

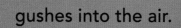

After hundreds of years
and billions of people burning fuels,
there's too much carbon in the air!

A blanket of too much carbon
is trapping too much heat in our skies,
warming oceans, melting glaciers,

causing storms
and floods

and drought
and fire.

But . . .

the Earth can help repair the air.
To scrub out carbon *up there*,

our planet has amazing powers
down here—

in the sea,

at the shore,

and on land.

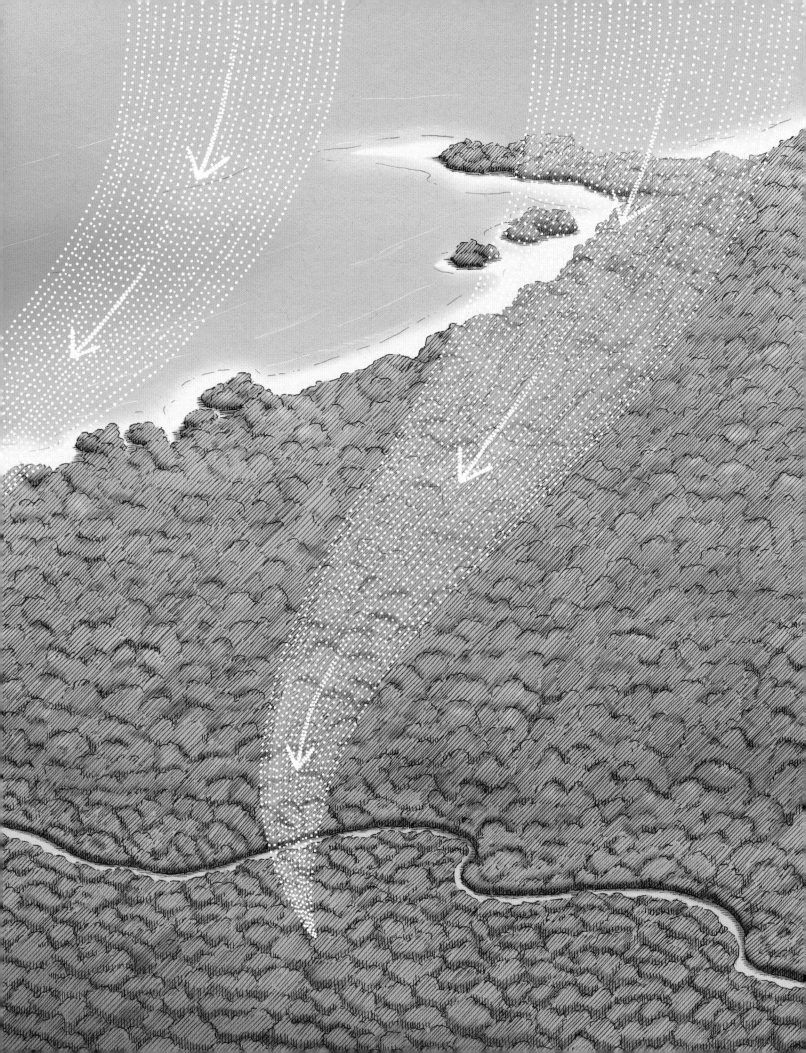

The Earth has the power of
kelp—
seaweed!—
in fast-growing underwater forests.

A blade of kelp, like a leaf, gulps down carbon
that the ocean has sucked from the air above
until the blade breaks off,
floats away, and sinks,
dragging the carbon it guzzled
to the bottom of the sea.

And—*also!*—

kelp forests shield shorelines from destructive ocean waves.

Kelp shelters shellfish and finfish and other sea critters.

Kelp can be good for eating!

Shielding, sheltering, feeding,
air-repairing kelp
can help and help and help,
one blade after another.

From sea to shore, the Earth has the power of
mangroves,
sturdy shrubby trees with wet feet
crowded into swampy stands.

Mangrove leaves soak up carbon from the air.

Roots, tough and twisty,
pull the carbon into the boggy floor,

where it's
captured!—
swallowed in mud.

And—

extra!—

with their roots piled up on roots,
mangroves trap silt and sediment,

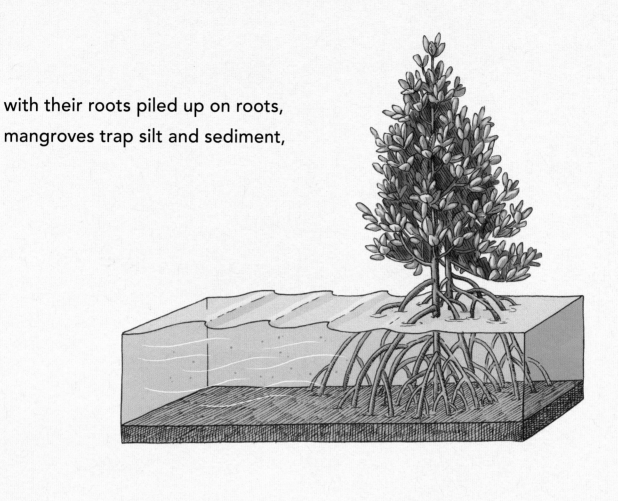

building up dirt,
building new wetlands,

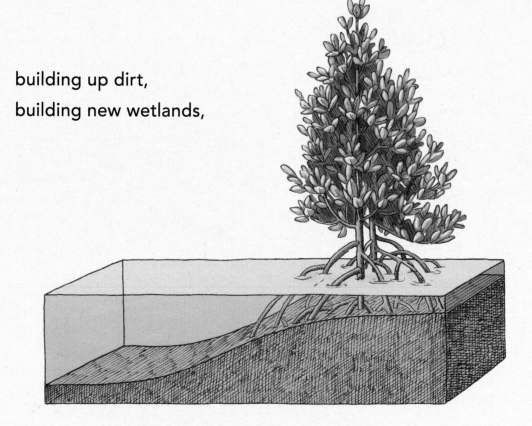

building barriers that protect our coastlines and our homes—
all while repairing the air,
one bundle of tangled roots at a time.

From shore to land, the Earth has the power of
dirt,
rich, dark, and damp soil
anchoring trees and grasses
and flowers and food crops.

Leaves drink carbon
from the air,

while roots reach down into the dirt,
burying countless sips of carbon
in the ground.

And—*bonus!*—

the more carbon pulled underground,
the healthier the dirt becomes.

The healthier the dirt—
soft, spongy, and carbon-stuffed—
the better for meadows and woodlands,
the better for farming and for gardening,

the better for giving us green spaces
and good foods,
one clump of dirt at a time.

At sea, by the shore, on land,
the Earth's powers are mighty.
But they are not enough.
There is too much carbon in the air
for the Earth to repair by itself.

For the Earth to keep helping us,
we must help the Earth.
And **people** have amazing powers to do that.

People have the power to **change**

from power stations that burn fossil fuels

from farms that disturb carbon-rich soil

from going places this way

to power stations that don't,

to farms that don't,

to getting there like this.

People have the power to **protect.**

People have the power to **invent.**
We have the power of **science!**

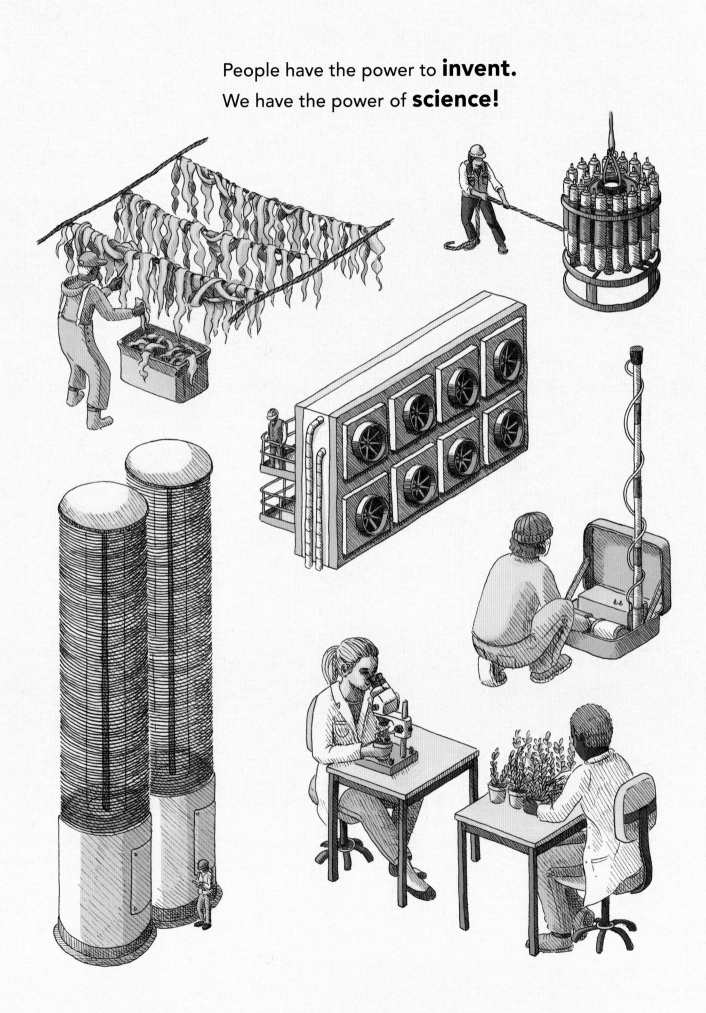

Yes, there's too much carbon in the air.
But the Earth,
and we people of the Earth,
have the power to make this better,
together.

AUTHOR'S NOTE

THE PROBLEM

You can't see it or smell it, but carbon is in the air all around us. It takes the form of carbon dioxide, also known as CO_2. Scientists have instruments that measure the amount of CO_2 in the atmosphere, and that amount has never been higher in human history.

Some carbon dioxide exists in the air naturally. But the high levels of CO_2 that our world is now experiencing didn't happen naturally. They are the result of something people have been doing for a long time: burning coal, oil, and gas.

Of course, the use of these fossil fuels has changed our lives in greatly beneficial ways. We easily heat and cool our buildings. We drive and fly places! We flip a switch and light up the night. We plug in and power up all kinds of machines.

But the benefits have a cost. All that excess CO_2 has caused the Earth's atmosphere to trap too much of the sun's heat. Our climate has changed. Many places are becoming warmer. Some are becoming too dry and some too wet. These changes are causing drought, wildfires, violent storms, and floods. Animals and plants are endangered by climate change. So are we humans.

THE POWERS

The Earth has amazing powers to heal. As you know from reading this book, kelp, mangroves, and dirt are able to heal the Earth by removing carbon dioxide from the atmosphere and oceans. But, as you also now understand, our planet's atmosphere has trapped so much CO_2 that these and other natural CO_2 absorbers, such as

trees, can't clean it up by themselves. So people are working to help the Earth help us, with projects like these:

- Communities are preserving and restoring mangrove, marsh, and kelp ecosystems.
- Aqua farmers are growing carbon-absorbing kelp in the ocean.
- Scientists are experimenting to create plants with deeper, stronger roots that can store carbon underground even more efficiently.
- Farmers are planting cover crops, so their fields always have carbon-storing roots anchored in the soil.

Then there are the people who are building machines to vacuum carbon dioxide right out of the air. Others are designing devices to draw carbon from the ocean—where too much CO_2 is harming sea life such as corals—and turn it into limestone!

Turning CO_2 into stone and vacuuming it out of the air are big, bold ideas we all can hope will succeed. But while efforts to protect and invent our way out of the CO_2 problem are important, they must be coupled with big reductions in the amount of carbon dioxide we add to the air. Manufacturers and agricultural companies can reduce their carbon dioxide emissions by changing the ways they make their products. Power companies can build more plants that generate electricity using alternatives to fossil fuels. Governments can encourage these changes through laws. Individuals can choose climate-friendly products. We can contact business and political leaders and tell them we want change. We can share accurate information about climate change.

There are other ways, too, in which people are pitching in to limit carbon dioxide:

- They're riding bicycles and battery-powered vehicles instead of driving CO_2-emitting cars to work and school.
- In sunny areas, they're putting solar panels on their roofs instead of using electricity generated by coal-fired power plants.

- They're running air conditioners less in the summer and furnaces less in the winter.

- They're having fun in no-till gardens growing flowers, vegetables, and fruits without turning over the dirt—allowing carbon to stay fixed in the ground.

- And they're eating more finfish, shellfish, and edible seaweeds (like kelp!), the harvesting of which can emit less CO_2 and use fewer resources than land-based foods such as beef cattle.

What will *you* do to help the Earth help us?

SELECTED SOURCES

Many references and resources were consulted in writing this book. What follows is a small sampling.

ABC News. "How an underwater solution in the Faroe Islands could combat climate change." November 3, 2021. https://abcnews.go.com/International/video/underwater-solution-faroe-islands-combat-climate-change-80963182.

Berhe, Asmeret Asefaw, PhD, professor, University of California, Merced; Falasco Chair in Earth Sciences and Geology. Interviewed by Debbie Levy, September 17, 2021.

———. "A climate change solution that's right under our feet." TED2019. April 2019. https://www.ted.com/speakers/asmeret_berhe.

The Blue Carbon Initiative (website). https://www.thebluecarboninitiative.org/.

Chapman, Samantha K., PhD, professor, Villanova University; codirector, Center for Biodiversity and Ecosystem Stewardship. Interviewed by Debbie Levy, September 20, 2021.

———. "Mangroves protect coastlines, store carbon—and are expanding with climate change." The Conversation, February 9, 2018. https://theconversation.com/mangroves-protect-coastlines-store-carbon-and-are-expanding-with-climate-change-81445.

CLEAR Center (website). Clarity and Leadership for Environmental Awareness and Research at University of California, Davis. https://clear.ucdavis.edu.

Conservation International. "Stabilizing our climate by protecting and restoring nature." https://www.conservation.org/priorities/stabilizing-our-climate-by-protecting-and-restoring-nature.

Flannery, Tim. "How farming giant seaweed can feed fish and fix the climate." The Conversation, July 31, 2017. https://theconversation.com/how-farming-giant-seaweed-can-feed-fish-and-fix-the-climate-81761.

Froehlich, Halley, PhD, assistant professor, University of California, Santa Barbara. Interviewed by Debbie Levy, October 6, 2021.

Gerretsen, Isabelle. "The remarkable power of Australian kelp." BBC Future Planet. April 14, 2021. https://www.bbc.com/future/article/20210406-how-kelp-can-help-solve-climate-change.

Gordon, Melissa. "The ocean farmers trying to save the world with seaweed." *Time*. September 4, 2020. https://time.com/5848994/seaweed-climate-change-solution/.

Kaplan, Sarah. "Humanity's greatest ally against climate change is Earth itself." *Washington Post*. April 22, 2021. https://www.washingtonpost.com/climate-solutions/2021/04/22/earth-day-biodiversity/.

Kiss the Ground (website and documentary film). https://kisstheground.com/.

Moritz, Bailey, program officer, aquaculture, World Wildlife Fund. Interviewed by Debbie Levy, March 31, 2022.

Salk Institute. Harnessing Plants Initiative (website). https://www.salk.edu/harnessing-plants-initiative/.

Spalding, M., A. McIvor, F. H. Tonneijck, and P. Eijk. "Mangroves for coastal defence." Wetlands International and the Nature Conservancy. 2014. https://www.nature.org/media/oceansandcoasts/mangroves-for-coastal-defence.pdf.

SubMERG (Sub-Tidal Marine Ecology Research Group) Lab (website). https://www.submerg.org/.

HOW ARE WE HELPING THE EARTH HELP US?

WE ARE CHANGING!

We are getting around by electric vehicles, public transportation, bicycles, and walking—which means fewer gas-powered, CO_2-emitting cars.

We are eating more finfish, shellfish, and edible seaweed. Harvesting these healthy and tasty foods from the ocean and other waterways can produce fewer greenhouse gas emissions than raising livestock for food.

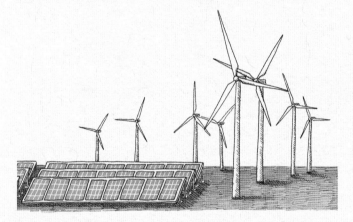

By generating electricity from solar and wind power instead of fossil fuels, we get more energy with fewer CO_2 emissions.

We are growing food crops in ways that keep more carbon buried in the soil.

WE ARE PROTECTING!

When we preserve and restore carbon-absorbing habitats, such as marshes and woodlands and mangrove forests, we give the Earth more chances to exercise its own amazing powers to repair the air.

reforestation and planting trees

PROTECTED WETLANDS

protecting existing green space